Time Code for Academic Excellence: Effective Time Management for Undergraduates.

By Charles Thompson.

Copyright@2024. Charles Thompson.

All rights reserved.

Table of content.

1. Prioritizing Academic Commitments: Strategies for Success

Explore methods for identifying and prioritizing academic tasks to ensure that essential assignments are completed on time.

2. Mastering the Pomodoro Technique: Boosting Productivity in Short Bursts

Dive into the Pomodoro Technique and its application to undergraduate studies, helping students maximize focus and productivity.

3. Striking a Balance: Juggling Academics, Extracurriculars, and Social Life

Discuss how to maintain a healthy balance between academic responsibilities, involvement in extracurricular activities, and socializing for a well-rounded undergraduate experience.

4. Effective Goal Setting: A Key to Time Management Success

Explore the process of setting SMART goals to guide undergraduates in managing their time efficiently and achieving academic milestones.

5. The Role of Technology in Time Management: Tools and Apps for Success

Investigate various technological tools and apps that can assist undergraduates in organizing their schedules, setting reminders, and enhancing overall time management.

6. Creating a Personalized Study Schedule: Tailoring Time Management to Your Needs.

Provide insights into designing individualized study schedules that align with personal learning preferences and peak productivity times.

7.Overcoming Procrastination: Strategies to Stay on Track

Delve into common causes of procrastination among undergraduates and offer practical strategies to overcome this challenge and maintain a proactive approach to time management.

8.Building Healthy Habits: Integrating Self-Care into Your Routine

Emphasize the importance of self-care in maintaining overall well-being, and discuss how incorporating healthy habits can contribute to effective time management.

9.Reflecting and Adapting: Continuous Improvement in Time Management

Encourage undergraduates to regularly reflect on their time management strategies, identify areas for improvement, and adapt their approaches to enhance overall efficiency and effectiveness.

INTRODUCTION:

The quest for scholarly greatness is a diverse excursion that requests commitment and difficult work as well as successful using time effectively and prioritization abilities. Understudies frequently wind-up wrestling with a plenty of scholastic undertakings, from tasks and tests to projects and extracurricular exercises. In this complicated snare of liabilities, the capacity to distinguish and focus on scholarly responsibilities becomes principal for progress. This article dives into exhaustive systems for knowing and positioning scholastic undertakings, guaranteeing that fundamental tasks are finished as well as finished with greatness and reliability.

CHAPTER ONE

Prioritizing Academic Commitments: Strategies for Success.

To explore the maze of scholarly obligations, it is basic to initially fathom the assorted idea of undertakings that understudies experience. Scholarly responsibilities include a range of exercises, going from day-to-day schoolwork tasks to significant exploration projects. Perceiving the differing levels of significance, time awareness, and individual fitness expected for each undertaking is key to successful prioritization.

Lay out Clear Objectives and Goals:

The groundwork of viable prioritization lies in laying out clear objectives and goals. Characterize present moment and long-haul scholarly objectives, adjusting them to you in general instructive desires. By having a clear-cut guide, you can without much of a stretch distinguish undertakings that contribute straightforwardly to your scholastic targets. This lucidity fills in as a compass, directing you in focusing on tasks that line up with your general objectives.

Separate Assignments into Reasonable Parts:

Huge tasks or activities frequently instigate pressure because of their apparently unfavorable nature. To defeat this, separate complex errands into more modest, more sensible parts. By analyzing tasks into more modest advances, you can assign time and assets productively, making it simpler to focus on each section in light of its importance and cutoff time.

Sort Undertakings In light of Significance and Criticalness:

The Eisenhower Box, a time usage instrument credited to President Dwight D. Eisenhower, characterizes assignments into four quadrants in light of their direness and significance. Quadrant I contains critical and fundamental errands, while Quadrant II incorporates significant however not dire assignments. Quadrants III and IV include undertakings that are either dire however not significant or neither critical nor significant. Applying this structure can help with classifying scholarly responsibilities, taking into consideration a methodical way to deal with prioritization.

Evaluate Individual Qualities and Shortcomings:

Understanding your assets and shortcomings is essential in focusing on scholarly errands. Recognize subjects or sorts of tasks where you succeed and those that posture difficulties. Focus on undertakings that line up with your assets, permitting you to proficiently benefit from your capacities and complete tasks more. All the while, designate extra time and assets to undertakings that challenge you, guaranteeing a decent and balanced way to deal with your scholastic responsibilities.

Time Usage Strategies:

Compelling prioritization is naturally connected to capable using time productively. Executing dependable strategies can fundamentally upgrade your capacity to apportion time reasonably to different scholarly errands.

Pomodoro Method:

The Pomodoro Method includes separating work into spans, generally 25 minutes long, isolated by brief breaks. In the wake of finishing four spans, enjoy some time off. This technique assists in keeping up with centering and efficiency by making a need to get moving during the work spans. Applying this procedure to scholastic responsibilities can support focusing on errands inside unambiguous time spans, upgrading by and large proficiency.

Time Hindering:

Time hindering includes booking explicit blocks of time for various undertakings. Designate devoted schedule openings for considering, going to classes, finishing tasks, and taking part in extracurricular exercises. By compartmentalizing your day, you can focus on assignments without feeling overpowered, guaranteeing that every part of your scholastic life gets the consideration it merits.

The 2-Minute Rule:

In the event that an undertaking takes under two minutes to finish, do it right away. This standard, instituted by efficiency master David Allen, is a basic yet strong methodology for overseeing more modest undertakings speedily. By tending to speedy assignments right away, you keep them from amassing and upsetting your emphasis on additional huge scholastic responsibilities.

Systems for Distinguishing Errand Need:

Once outfitted with a strong comprehension of the idea of scholarly responsibilities and furnished with compelling time usage methods, the following stage is leveling up the ability of distinguishing task need. A few systems can help with this interaction.

Assess Task Weightage:

Tasks and evaluations frequently convey different weightage regarding reviewing. Focus on assignments with higher weightage, guaranteeing that your endeavors contribute altogether to your general scholastic presentation. Notwithstanding, don't disregard lower-weightage undertakings completely, as they all in all add to a balanced presentation.

Think about Cutoff times and Time Responsiveness:

Time responsiveness is a basic figure deciding undertaking need. Assess the cutoff times for every task or project and focus on those with inescapable due dates. This guarantees that you comply with time constraints as well as designate adequate time for careful readiness and top-notch yield.

Adjust Assignments to Learning Goals:

Each scholastic assignment is intended to add to explicit learning goals. Focus on undertakings that adjust intimately with the course's center ideas and your own learning objectives. This essential methodology guarantees that you develop how you might interpret fundamental ideas while succeeding in tasks that straightforwardly add to scholarly achievement.

Look for Direction from Teachers:

Teachers act as important assets in exploring scholarly needs. Assuming you experience difficulties in deciding the meaning of undertakings or battle with prioritization, look for direction from your teachers or educators. They can give bits of knowledge into the educational plan's central places and deal exhortation on focusing on tasks successfully.

Adjusting Scholastic and Individual Responsibilities:

While succeeding scholastically is vital, finding some kind of harmony among scholarly and individual commitments is similarly significant. Ignoring individual prosperity and extracurricular exercises can prompt burnout and obstruct in general scholarly execution. Subsequently, consider the accompanying systems for keeping a good overall arrangement:

Focus on Taking care of oneself:

Chasing scholastic greatness, taking care of oneself frequently assumes a lower priority. Be that as it may, disregarding physical and mental prosperity can antagonistically influence your capacity to scholastically perform. Focus on sufficient rest, nutritious feasts, and ordinary activity to guarantee areas of strength for a for scholastic achievement.

Set Reasonable Assumptions:

Setting reasonable assumptions is fundamental in forestalling overpower. Figure out your restrictions and put forth attainable objectives. While scholastic goals are honorable, it's critical to find some kind of harmony among desire and plausibility to keep a practical speed all through the scholarly excursion.

Embrace a Development Mentality:

A development mentality involves seeing difficulties as any open doors for development instead of unrealistic deterrents. Embrace the mentality that scholastic difficulties are essential for the growing experience, cultivating strength and flexibility. This point of view empowers you to move toward undertakings with an uplifting perspective, upgrading your general scholarly experience.

Designate Time for Extracurricular Exercises:

Extracurricular exercises assume a crucial part in self-improvement and balanced training. Allot explicit schedule openings for side interests, sports, or different exercises that give pleasure and equilibrium to your life. Taking part in different pursuits adds to a comprehensive and enhanced scholarly experience.

CAUTION:

Focusing on scholastic responsibilities is a workmanship that consolidates mindfulness, powerful using time productively, and an essential way to deal with task recognizable proof. By laying out clear objectives, separating errands, and ordering tasks in view of earnestness and significance, understudies can explore the scholastic scene with artfulness. Executing time usage procedures, for example, the Pomodoro Strategy and time obstructing upgrades efficiency, while techniques like assessing task weightage and looking for direction from educators refine the method involved with recognizing task need.

CHAPTER TWO

Mastering the Pomodoro Technique: Boosting Productivity in Short Bursts.

In the domain of time usage methodologies, the Pomodoro Strategy remains as a guide of effectiveness, offering a direct yet strong way to deal with supporting efficiency. Starting in the last part of the 1980s, this procedure, created by Francesco Cirillo, has gathered boundless praise for its effortlessness and adequacy. By separating work into centered spans, regularly alluded to as "Pomodoros," sprinkled with brief breaks, people can develop uplifted fixation, relieve burnout, and accomplish more quicker than expected.

Setting out on the Pomodoro Cycle:

A standard Pomodoro involves 25 minutes of concentrated work observed by a short 5-minute relief.

In the wake of finishing four Pomodoros, enjoy a more stretched out break traversing 15 to 30 minutes.

This cyclic design finds some kind of harmony between serious concentration and essential restoration.

Objective Setting and Assignment Prioritization:

Before beginning a Pomodoro meeting, portray the errands on your plan.

Focus on assignments in view of direness and importance.

Separating bigger assignments into sensible portions renders them more congenial and reachable.

Limiting Interruptions:

Quietness notices and make a devoted work area to diminish disturbances.

The Pomodoro Method advocates for profound focus during work spans, a urgent part of ideal efficiency.

Altering Pomodoro to Suit Individual Preferences:

While the traditional 25/5 Pomodoro proportion reverberates with many, people can change stretches to line up with individual inclinations and errand requests.

Trying different things with various time spans works with the disclosure of an ideal working cadence.

Utilizing Apparatuses and Applications:

A variety of applications and apparatuses is custom-made to improve the Pomodoro Strategy experience.

Clock applications, task the executive's apparatuses, and efficiency trackers act as significant guides in remaining on track and dissecting execution patterns.

The Productive Advantages of Pomodoro:

Intensified Concentration and Focus:

Organized spans under the Pomodoro Strategy encourage supported consideration, bringing about greater work inside compacted time spans.

Combatting Stalling:

By taking apart work into reasonable sections, the Pomodoro Method destroys the mental hindrances adding to lingering.

Assignments become less overpowering, decreasing the inclination for hesitation.

Effective Using time effectively:

Setting exact time limits for assignments improves time portion productivity.

The need to get moving developed by the Pomodoro Method inspires people to finish jobs inside assigned time spans.

Making preparations for Burnout:

Customary breaks go about as a rampart against burnout and mental exhaustion, taking into consideration supported undeniable level efficiency over the course of the day.

Encouraging Work-Life Amicability:

Underlining the significance of breaks, the Pomodoro Procedure adds to a better balance between serious and fun activities.

Coordinating brief breaks into the working day advances generally speaking prosperity and stress decrease.

Restraining Interferences:

Teach partners and relatives about your Pomodoro timetable to limit interferences.

Instruments like outside sound blocking earphones can establish a climate helpful for centered work.

Adaptability as a Goodness:

While the Pomodoro Strategy is an intense efficiency device, adaptability is vital.

Change the strategy in view of undertaking necessities and individual inclinations.

Consistent Investigation and Transformation:

Consistently assess efficiency utilizing the Pomodoro Procedure.

Adjust work and break stretches in view of perceptions to tweak and enhance your work process.

Dominating the Pomodoro Strategy is a workmanship that reaches out past simple timekeeping. It includes a promise to the standards of centered work, normal breaks, and constant refinement. Via consistently coordinating this strategy into your day-to-day daily practice and fitting it to your special inclinations, you can open a huge flood in efficiency, empowering you to accomplish your objectives with more prominent productivity and fulfillment.

The strategy is broadly utilized and has shown to be useful for understudies in different ways. The following are a couple of instances of how the Pomodoro Strategy has helped understudies, in actuality:

Expanded Concentration and Efficiency:

Model: An understudy battling to focus on reading up for extensive stretches could take on the Pomodoro Method. By breaking their review meetings into sensible 25-

minute spans, they can keep up with more elevated levels of concentration and efficiency during every meeting.

Forestalling Burnout:

Model: During test readiness, an understudy could feel overpowered and focused. The Pomodoro Strategy forestalls burnout by integrating customary breaks, permitting the understudy to re-energize and keep a more practical amount of exertion all through the review period.

Time Mindfulness and Arranging:

Model: Understudies frequently underrate or misjudge the time expected for errands. Utilizing the Pomodoro Strategy assists them with fostering a superior comprehension of what amount of time undertakings really require. This better time mindfulness considers more reasonable preparation and booking of study meetings.

Upgraded Undertaking The executives:

Model: An understudy with various tasks and undertakings could find it trying to focus on errands. The Pomodoro Method supports separating enormous undertakings into more modest, more reasonable portions. This makes it simpler to handle individual parts and track progress all the more successfully.

Further developed Time Assessment:

Model: While chipping away at tasks, understudies could battle to gauge how long they need to finish each job. The Pomodoro Method helps in fostering a feeling of time and assessing the number of "Pomodoros" (work stretches) are required for various sorts of exercises.

Diminished Tarrying:

Model: Dawdling is really difficult for understudies. Realizing that a break is not far off can make it more straightforward for understudies to conquer the underlying protection from beginning an errand. The Pomodoro Strategy goes about as an organized way to deal with progressively gather speed.

Better Balance between fun and serious activities:

Model: Understudies frequently have various obligations, including scholarly work, extracurricular exercises, and individual life. The Pomodoro Strategy keeps an equilibrium by furnishing organized work spans with assigned breaks, permitting time for different parts of life.

Expanded Inspiration:

Model: Finishing a bunch of Pomodoros and seeing unmistakable improvement can spur. The pride after each engaged span urges understudies to reliably work.

Generally speaking, the Pomodoro Method has shown to be an important device for understudies by advancing concentration, using time effectively, and efficiency while likewise relieving the adverse consequences of burnout and lingering.

CHAPTER THREE

Striking a Balance: Juggling Academics, Extracurriculars, and Social Life.

A good arrangement of scholastics and extracurricular exercises is critical to an effective school insight. An awkwardness causes horrible showing in one region yet can prompt pressure and tension in both. The following are four hints in shuffling scholastics with extracurriculars.

Academics Come First

While extracurricular exercises are significant, scholastics start things out. Your most memorable obligation is getting those high grades and advancing all you can from your classes - the essential justification behind attending a university is to take classes and do well in them! It isn't sufficient to simply excel on the tests; you should get familiar with the material to have the option to apply it subsequent to moving on from school.

Foster a Timetable

Plan out what should be finished and when it should be done. Focus on your exercises so you leave nothing significant for last. While booking, make certain to plan around your classes and make certain to leave a lot of concentrating on time prior to booking extracurriculars.

Be Demanding about Extracurricular Exercises

Try not to join each club or association your grounds offer - it will be a major channel on your time and odds are good that you will not be keen on the greater part of them. Pick admirably among those you are genuinely inspired by and those that will help you while heading to progress. It is ideal to pick something like three or four exercises and spotlight on them through getting administrative roles.

Enjoy Reprieves

While getting an A on a test is an incredible objective, don't go overboard. A lot reading up particularly for extensive stretches of time is similarly as terrible as excessively little. Concentrate on in fragments of 45 minutes to an hour with a break of five to ten minutes. Get some margin to extend and re-energize with a bite. This assists you with keeping up with focus level and guarantees greatest maintenance of material.

A reasonable and effective harmony among scholastics and extracurricular exercises is fundamental for an understudy's life. It shows you ideas that go past the study hall's four walls. In a student driven homeroom, co-curricular exercises are critical to get a fruitful instructive encounter. These exercises which shift from partaking in actual schooling to learning music, develop significant fundamental abilities that an understudy can use until the end of their life.

Understudies are feeling the squeeze to improve in this exceptionally cutthroat society, accordingly finding some kind of harmony and become capable at using time effectively is basic. Keeping an exceptional harmony among scholastics and extra-curricular can assist with molding one's character and changes abilities into capacities.

For figuring out how to be practical and dependable giving equivalent weightage to scholastics and co-curricular exercises is the far ahead. Adjusting the two things has just gotten more enthusiastically in light of the serious climate. To adhere to a multi-layered approach and to harvest wanted results, finding some kind of harmony between activities is significant. To assist understudies with handling this tension we are posting a portion of the fundamental tips that can assist you with accomplishing the right sort of harmony among scholastics and co-curricular exercises.

As you leave on any extracurricular action being shrewd in picking them is fundamental. Except if you are energetic or feel sure to take part in that action you want to explore that prior to joining each and all that is presented in your area. You could in fact look for counsel from elderly folks on the most proficient method to seek after your inclinations while finding some kind of harmony in your scholastics. Pick exercises so that improve your scholastics and even offers you a stage to communicate your thoughts. Or, more than likely your character and certainty will be depleted and you might try and risk your scholarly objectives.

As we have seen above taking part in new exercises and learning new things is great except if we focus on what's significant and sort out ourselves. Laying out objectives empowers us to prompt all-encompassing turn of events and without a doubt supports expanding efficiency.

Leaving on the excursion of advanced education is a thrilling and extraordinary experience, set apart by scholastic difficulties, various extracurricular open doors, and the fashioning of deep-rooted companionships.

Accomplishing a balanced undergrad experience includes exploring the sensitive harmony between scholastic obligations, contribution in extracurricular exercises, and mingling. In this article, we will investigate procedures to keep up with harmony and take full advantage of your school years.

1. Focus on and put together:

The most vital phase in accomplishing balance is to focus on your responsibilities. Grasp your scholastic responsibility and distribute time as needs be. Make a week after week plan that incorporates committed concentrate on hours, class participation, and time for tasks. Focusing on undertakings will assist you with remaining coordinated and stay away from last-minute pressure.

2. Put forth Sensible Objectives:

While aspiration is honorable, laying out reasonable goals is essential. Recognize your cutoff points and be aware of your scholar and individual limit. Laying out reachable targets guarantees that you keep a good overall arrangement without undermining your prosperity.

3. **Using time productively**:

Using time productively is an expertise that can represent the moment of truth your school insight. Figure out how to enhance your time actually by breaking errands into more modest, sensible pieces. Use apparatuses, for example, organizers or computerized schedules to follow cutoff times and responsibilities. Compelling using time productively permits you to satisfy scholastic obligations without forfeiting extracurriculars and mingling.

4. **Select Significant Extracurriculars**:

While it very well might be enticing to join each club and association, more valuable to pick extracurricular exercises line up with your interests and objectives. Higher standards without ever compromising is vital. Being effectively taken part in a couple of significant exercises considers a seriously improving encounter without overpowering your timetable.

5. Fabricate an Emotionally supportive network:

Encircle yourself with a steady organization of companions, coaches, and counsels. These people can give direction, share encounters, and proposition significant bits of knowledge. A solid emotionally supportive network can assist you with exploring difficulties, both intellectual and individual, cultivating a feeling of having a place and lessening pressure.

6. **Practice Taking care of oneself:**

Recollect that taking care of oneself is a vital piece of keeping up with balance. Focus on your psychological and actual prosperity by getting sufficient rest, practicing consistently, and enjoying reprieves when required. A sound, very much refreshed mind is more useful and better prepared to deal with the requests of school life.

7. **Powerful Correspondence:**

Openness is absolutely vital while shuffling various responsibilities. Illuminate teachers, friends, and colleagues about your timetable and responsibilities. Being straightforward about your accessibility takes into account understanding and backing from people around you.

8. **Higher expectations no matter what in Mingling:**

While mingling is a fundamental part of the school insight, finding some kind of harmony is significant. Center around significant associations as opposed to the sheer amount of social communications. Quality companionships contribute fundamentally to a satisfying undergrad experience.

9. **Reflect and Change:**

Routinely evaluate your timetable and responsibilities. Consider what's functioning admirably and what needs change. Reconsider and make changes as important to keep up with balance and guarantee a positive and balanced school insight.

Conclusion

Accomplishing an amicable harmony between scholastic obligations, extracurricular inclusion, and mingling requires cautious preparation, mindfulness, and versatility. By focusing on, overseeing time successfully, and embracing taking care of oneself, you can make an undergrad experience that isn't just scholastically fulfilling yet in addition specifically satisfying and paramount. Take a stab at balance, remain consistent with your interests, and capitalize on the extraordinary excursion that is school life.

CHAPTER FOUR

Effective Goal Setting: A Key to Time Management Success.

SMART goals are explicit, quantifiable and noteworthy. By utilizing a progression of five benchmarks that involve the Savvy strategy, you'll have the option to make succinct objectives and activity steps that will keep you on target.

How might explicit objectives have an effect? Think about this illustration of an obscure objective, and how this equivalent objective could be communicated subsequent to utilizing the Brilliant Technique:

Ambiguous objective: I need to assist my specialty with remaining on financial plan this year.

Shrewd objective: Every month, I will convey a financial plan report that shows our specialization's ongoing costs in contrast with our dispensed yearly spending plan and I will feature regions where we are overspending. In light of our ongoing spending, I will give thoughts on the most proficient method to cut expenses so we are back inside financial plan.

Your SMART goal is now something measurable and actionable with enough specifics to help you achieve real results. Keep reading to see exactly how we went from a vague goal to a SMART goal.

Instructions to define Brilliant objectives utilizing the Savvy technique

We should investigate the five parts of making a Shrewd objective.

1.**Make your goal SPECIFIC.**

The initial phase in making a Brilliant objective is to make it explicit. Think about your objective in quantifiable terms by posing yourself the accompanying inquiries:

What is it that I need to achieve?

Will accomplishing this objective have a significant effect?

What moves will I really want to make?

2. Make your goal MEASURABLE.

This moves toward the brilliant cycle prompts you to apply strategies for estimating your advancement toward accomplishing your objective. Being quantifiable additionally makes into account any moves you would execute to assist you with encouraging your advancement toward your objective. For example, this might appear as following the time it makes a you to finish a move or meet an achievement.

3. Make your goal ACHIEVABLE.

This part of the Savvy methodology connects with your objective being feasible. Do you have the assets and time expected to accomplish the objective? This might incorporate social event fundamental information, asking colleagues for help and mastering new abilities. You're bound to find success in your objective once it is explicit, quantifiable and considered reachable.

4. Make your goal RELEVANT.

A pertinent objective will straightforwardly add to victories. Remember that each activity you take ought to draw you nearer to your objective. In our model, an important objective will straightforwardly diminish costs.

Applying Shrewd "Significant" models: "I will convey a financial plan report that shows our specialization's ongoing costs in contrast with our dispensed yearly spending plan and I will feature regions where we are overspending. In light of our ongoing spending, I will give thoughts on the most proficient method to cut expenses so we are back inside financial plan."

5. **Make your goal TIME-BASED.**

A time sensitive objective makes some particular memories cutoff time. You'll need to decide whether your objective is a present moment or long haul objective (or a mix of both). From that point, you can decide a course of events and set a timetable to comply with time constraints and achieve your goal. Your timetable ought to likewise be sensible and permit you a lot of chances to make acclimations to your objective in regards to its significance, particularity and feasibility. Think about the last move toward the Shrewd cycle in the accompanying model.

Applying Brilliant "Time sensitive" models: "Every month in the current year, I will convey a spending plan report that shows our specialization's ongoing costs in contrast with our distributed yearly spending plan and I will feature regions where we are overspending. In view of our ongoing spending, I will give thoughts on the most proficient method to cut expenses so we are back inside financial plan."

Investigating the system of putting forth Shrewd objectives gives an organized structure that essentially improves an undergrad understudy's ability to effectively deal with their time and achieve scholarly achievements. Brilliant is an abbreviation indicating Explicit, Quantifiable, Feasible, Pertinent, and Time-bound — characteristics that render objectives clear, reachable, and centered. A more inside and out assessment of every part uncovers the accompanying experiences:

Explicit:

Understudies are encouraged to express their objectives with accuracy. As opposed to obscure goals, for example, "succeed in tests," particularity involves portraying the subject, section, or ability they plan to dominate.

Model: "Achieve A grade in the impending Measurements test by extensively understanding and applying speculation testing standards."

Quantifiable:

Objectives ought to be quantifiable for progress following. This includes integrating mathematical benchmarks or rates to measure accomplishments.

Model: "Complete all week-by-week readings for the semester, guaranteeing a careful comprehension and synopsis of something like 90% of the material."

Reachable:

While objectives ought to introduce difficulties, they should likewise be reasonable. Understudies are urged to assess their ongoing responsibility, accessible assets, and abilities to discover the feasibility of the objective inside given limitations.

Model: "Improve programming abilities by embraced a progression of coding activities and ventures this semester, representing other scholastic responsibilities."

Important:

Objectives should line up with more extensive intellectual and individual goals. Understudies ought to evaluate whether the objective is relevant to their course of study and long-haul yearnings.

Model: "Upgrade public talking abilities through dynamic cooperation in somewhere around two scholarly introductions this semester, lining up with the correspondence necessities of my picked field."

Time-bound:

Setting cutoff times infuses a need to get going, supporting understudies in keeping on track. Laying out a time period makes responsibility and helps with separating bigger objectives into sensible undertakings.

Model: "Close the draft of the examination paper toward the finish of Week 8, assigning fourteen days for modifications with maybe some time to spare."

Applying the Savvy rules to objectives gives understudies a reasonable guide for progress. This strategy works with successful using time productively as well as offers a system for nonstop assessment and change. Routinely returning to and refining Savvy objectives empowers understudies to keep focused, support inspiration, and celebrate steady victories on their scholastic process. A unique cycle develops mindfulness and key preparation, encouraging a proactive and objective situated way to deal with using time productively.

On the off chance that the Shrewd models are not followed, there are a few potential hindrances that people might experience in objective setting and using time effectively:

Dubiousness and Absence of Lucidity:

Without explicitness, objectives might need clear heading, making it trying to comprehend what should be accomplished. This can prompt disarray and an absence of inspiration.

Trouble in Estimation:

Without quantifiable models, progress won't be quickly followed. This makes it trying to decide how close or far one is from accomplishing the objective and can bring about an absence of responsibility.

Unreasonable Assumptions:

Neglecting to guarantee that objectives are feasible may prompt setting unreasonable assumptions. This can bring about disappointment, burnout, and a feeling of disappointment on the off chance that goals are impossible inside the given limitations.

Absence of Significance:

Objectives that are not pertinent to one's general targets or setting might redirect investment from significant pursuits. This absence of arrangement can prompt a feeling of disappointment and unfulfillment.

Stalling:

Objectives without time-bound cutoff times might be endlessly deferred, prompting lingering. The shortfall of a need to get going can impede progress and result in botched open doors.

Ineffectual Asset Allotment:

Neglecting to consider the accessible assets and requirements might bring about unfortunate asset allotment. This can prompt burnout or disregard of other significant obligations.

Absence of Inspiration:

Objectives that are not rousing or important may neglect to inspire people. Without a reasonable association with individual yearnings, people might battle to track down the drive to seek after and achieve their objectives.

Trouble in Arranging:

The shortfall of an obvious arrangement might make it trying to separate bigger objectives into sensible undertakings. This can bring about an absence of heading and a sensation of being overpowered.

Failure to Learn and Adjust:

Without an organized system for assessment, people might botch valuable chances to gain from their encounters and change their objectives likewise. This can upset individual and scholastic development.

Unfortunate Using time productively:

Ignoring the time-bound part of objectives might prompt unfortunate using time productively. This can bring about missed cutoff times, surged work, and a general lessening in the nature of execution.

In rundown, not following the Savvy standards can prompt various difficulties, including an absence of bearing, unfortunate advancement following, ridiculous assumptions, and troubles in remaining roused. Embracing the Savvy approach assists people with putting forth significant and reachable objectives, encouraging a more proficient and compelling way to progress.

The Role of Technology in Time Management: Tools and Apps for Success.

The Manner in which Innovation Has Impacted Using time effectively

It's a well-known fact that innovation can assist you with keeping focused and further develop your time usage abilities. Consider what amount of time it used to require to make an impression on somebody through the postal help versus the now moment satisfaction of email. Nonetheless, as you explore the effect of innovation on using time productively, you should likewise consider ways of guaranteeing that innovation doesn't hinder you. An internet-based time span mini-computer can help you alongside the innovation. Indeed, imagine a scenario where you had the option to deal with your errands in time. You can do that with the assistance of a clock number cruncher.

The most widely recognized analysis evened out at innovation and modern times is that they are time sinks that decrease efficiency and personal satisfaction. To be sure, it is entirely expected to get derailed in a labyrinth of hyperlinks and interruptions while dealing with an errand that started as an engaged, explicit, and time-bound try. The deception of performing multiple tasks as a computerized age "superpower" is inseparably connected to interruptions, unfortunate using time productively, and loss of efficiency. In any case, a period mini-computer empowers you to watch out for the creation.

Studies have found that computerized locals continually hop between various types of advanced media, about once consistently, diminishing their close to home interest in any action. This is the most widely recognized justification behind unfortunate using time productively. Yet, using time productively could be handily improved by utilizing an internet-based time adding machine. Organizations depend on the cloud and PC frameworks to guarantee project fruition. Moreover, online schedules have outperformed manual to-tackle task records. The main job of innovation is to save time and exertion. Innovation empowered instruments that save you a lot of time likewise work on in general proficiency and efficiency. Therefore, innovation and using time productively can be said to remain closely connected. In this article, you will become familiar with the job innovation plays in using time effectively.

1. **Use Innovation To Plan Your Day**

A fantastic time usage action is cautiously arranging your day. How frequently have we shown up by the day's end and pondered where it has gone? Getting some margin to arrange for how you will go through your day helps hold it back from getting endlessly. Innovation can help us in such manner. Online schedules help us in booking occasions and helping us to remember them with the goal that we don't miss them. These schedules might in fact be synchronized to your cell phone. Besides, a period length number cruncher can likewise furnish you with the office to diminish the time gambles with associated with the achievement of different errands.

Numerous internet-based schedules are assembled straightforwardly into the email clients we as of now use. You may just have to invest a little energy finding out about the elements of your program and how to utilize them for your potential benefit. Schedules and planning applications should indeed be easy to utilize and as undetectable as could be expected. On the off chance that they aren't, you won't utilize them since they burn through additional time than they save.

Online schedules can be an especially valuable time usage instrument for gatherings. Knowing when your colleagues have significant occasions arranged can assist with keeping away from pointless interferences. It can likewise support the association of gatherings and other gathering exercises. Additionally, time length mini-computers can help you to orchestrate your gatherings at the legitimate time.

Legitimate preparation is fundamental for capitalizing on any booking application, particularly on the off chance that you mean to involve it in a social scene. Invest some energy showing bunch individuals how to utilize the innovation. Set essential standard procedures for how the gathering will utilize the innovation with the goal that everybody grasps its importance.

Responsibility for time is a basic initial phase in fostering a time usage procedure. Then, at that point, it's simply a question of finding the right devices to help you in capitalizing on your 24-hour day. Make sure to explore different avenues regarding new advancements to find the instrument that turns out best for you.

2. Significantly having an impact on The Manner in which Organizations Convey

One of the incredible advantages of innovation is that it has changed correspondence norms. Cell phones, interpersonal interaction destinations, and talk applications give a better approach for speaking with incredible achievement. Correspondence of various levels has been presented with extraordinary achievement. Presently you can speak with your workers, educators, companions or various individuals easily.

Through person-to-person communication applications like WhatsApp, Skype, and others, you can send messages, message or video visit, or even have video gatherings with partners or bosses. It isn't important to be available in your work environment, you can be in contact with your work or business with the assistance of innovation. This is one of the extraordinary progressions in the area of innovation. You can chip away at other significant assignments beyond the workplace while keeping in contact with your collaborators by means of video visits and telephone calls. A period term number cruncher can likewise give you help in dealing with your web-based video call times so you experience no difficulty finishing your jobs.

3. Keep Your Routine Completely Coordinated

Innovation supports the association of the business. Project the board programming is an innovative instrument that helps keep your day-to-day errands completely coordinated. Likewise, the date span number cruncher is a productive instrument. Bosses and chiefs can without much of a stretch screen work environment exercise, which supports keeping everything on target. It lays out liability, responsibility, effectiveness, and opportune finishing of the undertakings relegated to people.

Numerous creative items and programming are presently accessible in the advanced work environment to further develop work process and productivity. Project the board programming is extremely useful to raise the quality and amount of work, and it likewise directs the results of wrong choices. It urges us to utilize innovation admirably to increase our expectation of living on the planet. It puts together all that and is the justification behind our brilliant future.

4. Utilizing Different Applications in Your Work

There are various applications accessible for figuring out how plans for the day and undertakings. An internet-based time mini-computer is one such device that is accessible. In the event that you as of now use Google Drive and other Google efficiency devices, you ought to check it out. It has very little highlights, yet the point of interaction is easy to utilize, and when joined with different applications, it tends to be a genuine resource.

Various technological tools and apps that can assist undergraduates in organizing their schedules, setting reminders, and enhancing overall time management.

In the quick moving and requesting universe of advanced education, powerful using time effectively is vital for progress. Students frequently wind up shuffling numerous classes, tasks, extracurricular exercises, and social responsibilities. To explore this intricacy and lift efficiency, different mechanical devices and applications have arisen to help understudies in coordinating their timetables, setting updates, and advancing in general using time productively. In this investigation, we will dive into a scope of these devices, looking at their elements, advantages, and how they add to the scholar and individual progress of students.

Schedule and Planning Applications:

a. Google Schedule:

Google Schedule is a flexible device that coordinates flawlessly with other Google administrations. It permits clients to make occasions, set updates, and offer timetables with peers. The application's easy to understand connection point and cross-stage accessibility make it a fundamental apparatus for understudies hoping to productively coordinate their scholar and individual lives.

b. Microsoft Viewpoint:

Standpoint gives vigorous planning and schedule highlights, empowering understudies to successfully deal with their time. Its joining with Microsoft Office Suite takes into consideration consistent progress between email, schedule, and efficiency applications, upgrading by and large productivity.

c. Apple Schedule:

For clients in the Apple biological system, the Apple Schedule application offers a direct connection point with highlights like variety coded occasions and iCloud synchronization. It is especially helpful for understudies who own Macintosh gadgets, guaranteeing a strong client experience across Macintosh, iPhone, and iPad.

Task The executives Applications:

a. Todoist:

Todoist is a famous errand the executives' application that permits understudies to make plans for the day, set cutoff times, and focus on undertakings. Its instinctive plan and coordinated effort highlights settle on it an incredible decision for bunch projects and shared liabilities.

b. Asana:

Asana is an undertaking the executive's device that can be adjusted for individual use or gathering projects. With highlights like errand task, due dates, and progress following, it assists understudies with remaining coordinated and guarantees that every individual from a gathering is in total agreement.

c. Trello:

Trello's card-based framework is great for visual students. Understudies can make sheets for various subjects or exercises and use cards to address errands. The simplified point of interaction makes it simple to move undertakings through various phases of finishing.

Note-Taking Applications:

a. Evernote:

Evernote is a thorough note-taking application that permits clients to catch and coordinate data in different configurations, including text, pictures, and sound. It is especially helpful for keeping address notes, exploration, and thoughts in one effectively open area.

b. OneNote:

Microsoft's OneNote is a computerized scratch pad that empowers understudies to take notes, draw charts, and team up with peers. Its coordination with other Microsoft Office applications makes it consistent for understudies previously utilizing the Workplace Suite.

c. Idea:

Idea is an across-the-board work area that joins note-taking, task the executives, and joint effort highlights. It offers an adaptable and adaptable stage for understudies to make a customized work area that suits their particular necessities.

Concentration and Efficiency Applications:

a. Timberland:

Timberland utilizes a one-of-a-kind idea to support efficiency. Client's plant virtual trees that develop over a set period, and assuming they utilize their telephone during that time, the tree bites the dust. This gamified approach assists understudies with keeping on track and stay away from interruptions.

b. StayFocusd:

StayFocusd is a program expansion that limits how much time clients can spend on diverting sites. This device is gainful for understudies who battle with tarrying and need a method for restricting time-squandering exercises during concentrate on meetings.

c. Pomodoro Clock Applications (e.g., Focus@Will, Be Engaged):

Pomodoro method applications break concentrate on meetings into short, engaged stretches (commonly 25 minutes), trailed by a brief break. These applications assist understudies with keeping up with focus, further develop using time productively, and forestall burnout during expanded concentrate on meetings.

Conclusion:

In the steadily developing scene of training, mechanical devices and applications assume an urgent part in helping students with using time effectively. Whether it's planning, task the board, note-taking, or improving concentration and efficiency, the range of instruments accessible guarantees that understudies can find an answer customized to their inclinations and requirements. By integrating these apparatuses into their everyday schedules, students can explore the intricacies of scholastic life all the more proficiently, at last adding to their prosperity and prosperity. As innovation keeps on propelling, what's to come holds considerably additional promising developments to additional help understudies in their instructive excursion.

CHAPTER SIX

Creating a Personalized Study Schedule: Tailoring Time Management to Your Needs.

What is Customized Realizing?

A Customized Learning is the customization and transformation of instructive strategies and procedures so the educational experience is more qualified for every individual student, with their own interesting learning style, foundation, needs, and past encounters.

Learning can occur in a heap of better places, exercises, techniques, and time periods.

From the auditorium populated with many students standing by listening to an educator to a one-on-one mentorship program, from intuitive internet games to complex specialized course readings, there are so many configurations that learning can take.

There are a wide range of learning procedures, as well as many styles of instructing and realizing, all of which consolidate to make each opportunity for growth unique and customized. Each kind of learning has advantages and disadvantages and will offer various things to various students.

In a customized learning approach, the student's very own insight, information, and propensities are associated with learning strategies, so they can learn quicker, see new ideas all the more effectively, and further develop their learning execution.

The easiest illustration of customized learning would be the point at which a teacher furnishes learning material with legitimate substance and setting, and in the most ideal way for the student.

This is finished by utilizing the current information that the educator has of the understudy. The educator comprehends how best to interface the student's past encounters and capacities to the new data, building joins between existing information and new data.

Appropriate learning material is content that is applicable to the student's past encounters.

The most ideal way, for every student, is conveyance of data so that the student can get the new data without any problem.

This could be the kind of material (video, text, or intuitive games, for instance), the time spent, how much material shrouded in every meeting, and the request wherein new data is made sense of. This will change for every student, as everybody has different learning styles.

This, obviously, is certainly not a versatile arrangement, yet it is the most straightforward clarification of how customized learning can be actioned. It is a course of association, of conveying the right devices to help the learning way.

These days, to get this kind of approach going, and all the more critically, be versatile, associations should have the option to make a computerized learning foundation that can robotize this cycle and make it financially savvy.

Why is customized learning significant?

If an association has any desire to further develop learning results, customized learning is a demonstrated method for doing as such.

By taking information connected with a student's past encounter and connecting that to new ideas, customized learning brings about a more complete comprehension of new ideas, better commitment, and information maintenance is gotten to the next level. So, customized learning makes learning more successful.

By taking a gander at the past model, you can perceive how customized learning can change a typical preparation program and make it more customized for every novel client. Such changes make the growing experience connecting with, quicker, and more viable.

In any event, making learning content marginally customized will have an effect, for instance, eliminating material that is pointless while featuring the preparation that will help the student most.

As innovation propels, students become seriously requesting, and they anticipate that preparing projects should keep up. These days, customized content is all over. We have customized benefits from online entertainment, individual playlists, film proposals, and a ton of different things. We as of now expect that any new apparatus will have something almost identical. At work, we expect that the learning stage will offer us a genuinely new thing, significant precisely for us.

Without refreshing how learning is conveyed, associations risk withdrawing representatives in an imperative region.

Not just that, look at what as another representative will believe in the event that they start their onboarding cycle with an organization that utilizes an obsolete, non-customized way to deal with preparing. Will they believe that this association can help them upskill all through their vocation? Will they treat the association in a serious way as a cutthroat and ground breaking organization to work for?

Representatives reliably report that they search for occupations that will offer preparation and potential open doors for development, and will remain longer in jobs that give them. As workers learn, they can work on their exhibition, conveying better business results.

Great worker preparing projects can increment income, help efficiency, and breed development inside an association. As additional associations face the test of upskilling laborers successfully and effectively, customized learning has come into the spotlight as a technique that can convey that in a versatile way.

Advantages of customized learning

1. Saves time

Customized learning eliminates the time it takes a student to draw in with and grasp another subject.

It additionally eliminates content that is at this point not pertinent or would be repetitive because of the experience level of the student, saving time that would somehow be squandered on learning ideas that won't serve the student.

2. Increments commitment

At the point when content is both significant and customized, learning is seriously captivating.

A student is bound to interface with, and recall content that objectives their ongoing job, tasks, or area of work.

3. Further develops information maintenance

At the point when content depends on past experience, the student will hold that data any more timeframe.

At the point when a customized learning way interfaces each piece of the riddle together, with each piece supporting each other to interlace the data, the student will actually want to all the more likely review data by connecting it to existing information.

4. Expanded inspiration

Discovering that is associated with something important, be it the student, their work, or their leisure activities will increment inspiration for the student.

This is particularly evident assuming the substance contains tips or accommodating data that is quickly significant.

5. Further develops learning results

Studies have shown that a customized learning approach yields better learning results. This approach raises learning and gives content that is applicable, connecting with, significant, and paramount.

The final product is a student who is satisfied with their cooperation with the material and is better at their particular employment.

Examples of personalized learning.

1. Tutoring

One of the notable methods of customized learning is tutoring. The more experienced representative is relegated as a counsel to the less experienced worker.

With all information that the tutor assembled by encountering something before, he could comprehend the issues and hardships that the mentee is confronting and guide the learning towards understanding.

This model works perfectly, however its restriction is in its versatility.

2. Online course suppliers

You have most certainly seen these kinds of courses, and likely utilized one yourself.

Coursera, edX, LinkedIn Learning, Open Sesame, and many, numerous others. In those administrations, you have an individual record that the framework tracks and stores all of your learning information to offer you new significant courses.

At the point when you get done with one course, the stage will offer you progressed courses or materials pertinent to the subject.

3. Web indexes

Web indexes are the most famous method of customized learning. Google responds to your inquiries with customized addresses.

Assuming you like to peruse, you could arrange books on the web, or visit some distribution locales to find another book, Google will recall that. So, assuming you google "Harry Potter", the framework will offer you the best proposals from online book shops. Simultaneously, on the off chance that you like to watch films, and do it regularly on the web, you will see film related replies.

Indeed, even the subject is something similar, "Harry Potter", Google realizes that the subject contains an alternate sort of data.

Information Chart, the innovation behind that, associates various parts of the subjects together.

Thus, eventually, you can see the outcomes that are generally pertinent to you. Harry Potter is a book, film, character, and you even will see pictures and profiles of Daniel Radcliffe, the entertainer who played the person.

All of this happened in light of the fact that Google needs to give the most important data to the clients as could be expected, and utilizes customized figuring out how to do as such.

4. Corporate preparation model

Air Techniques, a Colorado-based helicopter clinical vehicle organization utilized customized figuring out how to support their pilot preparing program.

Utilizing a cloud-based learning framework, they went to man-made consciousness to pinpoint the subjects in which pilots were battling and present more data and diversely phrased inquiries to guarantee that pilots genuinely knew the point.

By utilizing incessant, short tests and games, the pilots were locked in and the association was effectively ready to pinpoint regions where more preparation was required.

This utilization of customized learning permitted the organization to cut face to face, teacher drove instructional courses fifty, and furthermore decreased the quantity of days required for onboarding, from ten to five days.

How to make learning much more customized and successful

At the point when all that data about the representative is accessible to the personalization motor, it could make substantially more legitimate estimates about the pertinence of some data for the worker.

By examining the learning history, it could turn out to be clear what realizing design is generally appropriate for the individual. For instance, does perusing an article offer more to the learning than sound, do they favor longer learning meetings with expansive setting introduced or would it be a good idea for it to be short and straightforwardly to the subject, or do advancing necessities fluctuate contingent upon the hour of day or day of the week?

Much more important outcomes could be delivered when the worker's information and experience are contrasted with other representatives' encounters and similitudes tracked down in jobs, abilities, or learning exercises. Then, at that point, the importance of the data gave to the worker could be worked on in light of that likeness.

This likewise functions admirably for another representative who has no past history in an organization. From the get go, similitudes like job and division as well as a shortfall of past learning history could bring them pertinent onboarding materials, and afterward by dissecting the historical backdrop of the past rookies, a proposal motor will take care of the student with ideas that are now demonstrated to be pertinent to the individuals who traveled every which way through onboarding materials previously.

Obviously, it isn't the finish of the story, it is just barely the start. To carry it to a higher level, the circle should be shut and learning ought to be applied to the personalization motor to deliver better significance after some time. Breaking down learning exercises, checking what representatives were picking themselves from results proposed, inquiring as to whether they were happy with results given, investigating refined look - all that will cause the suggestion motor to improve and adjust constantly utilizing AI.

How to make a customized learning design

To appropriately saddle the force of this kind of data conveyance, a customized learning plan ought to be executed.

Customized learning plan is a record that incorporates the short and long-haul objectives of the student, covers their assets, shortcomings, abilities, and information holes, and sets out the learning plan that is best for that specific student. It is the guide that the student will follow to come to their instructive or preparing objectives.

1. Survey

A customized learning plan generally starts with an evaluation. To know where you need to go, you should know where you are beginning from!

Evaluations can be made for explicit jobs or at a group or departmental level and can be utilized for a few representatives simultaneously.

They ought to survey what data ought to be known, at what level, and ought to have the option to recognize explicit information holes.

When the student has finished their evaluation, this information can be input into the framework, and the improvement of a learning plan can start.

The equivalent is valid on a departmental and all-inclusive level. Information from groups can feature the weak spots in an office, and show where their assets are.

2. Decide the objectives and abilities required for every particular job

Since it has become so obvious where you are beginning from, you should next choose where you are going.

It ought to be resolved which abilities or skills are required for every job or division.

Thusly, an association can make or change learning materials to create or work on those abilities.

Objectives and abilities ought to be made by the Shrewd technique, with the goal that the students, or the offices, progress in contacting them can be all the more handily followed.

3. Make a conventional learning plan

You have assembled information on the ongoing level of worker's information and abilities, and recognized what they need to realize.

The subsequent stage is fostering the way to get them there. A learning plan ought to be created.

This needn't bother with to be hyper-explicit - a nonexclusive series of steps that take the student from point A to point B will get the job done, and information will be accumulated as additional students utilize this way to assist with customizing it for future students.

4. Map learning modalities

Attempting to comprehend how the student cooperates with learning materials, and which materials will turn out best for this specific individual is a significant part of customized learning.

Do they favor video content? Maybe they are more open to working with text and smaller than normal tests.

Every individual will have inclinations for how they draw in with the material, and this ought to be found at this step.

As it found turns out best for every individual, this data ought to be planned.

It is likewise great, at this stage, to make student profiles. This profile not exclusively can show the way of the singular student and their achievements; however, it can likewise act as an outline for different students in comparative jobs.

Understanding how every student has been fruitful can be important information for a preparation program.

5. Alter learning plans for people as indicated by their particular inclinations

By altering the learning plan, utilizing information about the student's particular information level, inclination of content, and numerous different elements, an association can guarantee that students are locked in, acquiring abilities, and not throwing away their energy on pointless substance.

6. Use appraisals to follow learning

Repeating registrations through appraisals ought to be executed to guarantee that the learning way is fruitful.

These evaluations, both one-on-one and self, ought to then convey information to be investigated that will assist with giving a window into the student's excursion.

One-on-one appraisals are significant here, as they consider criticism, critical thinking, objective rebuilding, and numerous other positive activities that can assist students with being upheld in arriving at their objectives.

A customized learning plan is driven by this information, and the more information that there is, the more responsive it tends to be.

7. Audit and scale

All through the program, the association ought to audit the cycle, consistently work to further develop the general student experience and ensure that the actual interaction is enhanced.

Conclusion

Making learning customized extraordinarily affects learning results. At the point when new ideas are connected to an individual's past encounter, it brings about better comprehension, and learning turns out to be more viable.

In a hierarchical climate, the formation of customized learning requires innovation answers for make it savvy and versatile.

Innovation, similar to a blend of Involvement Programming interface (xAPI) and Learning Record Store (LRS), empowers the assortment of a worker's encounters on an exceptionally granular level in computerized structure.

In the contemporary scholarly scene, where the requests on an undergrad understudy's time are complex, the mix of mechanical apparatuses and applications has become instrumental in smoothing out processes and upgrading by and large using time productively. This investigation digs into a different exhibit of these devices, carefully intended to help students in sorting out plans, setting updates, and at last sustaining their grip on powerful using time productively.

Using time productively is a basic expertise for students as they explore through a large number of scholarly obligations, extracurricular commitment, and individual responsibilities. Utilizing innovation in this setting offers a powerful arrangement, furnishing understudies with open and natural assets to assist them with capitalizing on their time.

One classification of apparatuses that has acquired unmistakable quality is planning and schedule applications. Stages like Google Schedule, Microsoft Viewpoint, and Apple Schedule offer understudies the capacity to make, sort out, and share their timetables flawlessly. These instruments take into consideration the contribution of class timings, task cutoff times, and other significant dates, giving a visual portrayal of the long stretches of time to come. Furthermore, they frequently coordinate with different applications, empowering understudies to set updates and get warnings for looming assignments. The capacity to get to these schedules across different gadgets guarantees that understudies have their timetables readily available, working with proficient preparation.

Task the executives' apparatuses address one more feature of the innovative stockpile accessible to students. Applications like Todoist, Trello, and Asana enable understudies to separate bigger tasks or activities into reasonable undertakings. This not just guides in making an organized way to deal with work yet additionally offers a feeling of achievement as errands are finished. These apparatuses frequently consolidate highlights like due dates, need levels, and progress following, empowering understudies to remain coordinated and zeroed in on their scholastic goals.

The important mix taking applications has additionally changed the manner in which students draw in with their coursework. Evernote, OneNote, and Thought are instances of stages that permit understudies to carefully assemble and coordinate their notes. The benefit lies in the openness and accessibility of notes, lessening the time spent filtering through actual materials. These applications frequently support media components, empowering understudies to incorporate sound accounts, pictures, and connections, making extensive and dynamic review assets.

To upgrade cooperative endeavors, distributed storage and record sharing administrations have demonstrated priceless. Google Drive, Dropbox, and Microsoft

OneDrive work with consistent cooperation on bunch projects and guarantee that reports are available whenever, anyplace. This advances proficient collaboration as well as mitigates the gamble of losing essential documents.

The domain of using time productively stretches out past preparation and association; it includes the requirement for concentration and fixation. Applications like Timberland and Focus@Will address this perspective by carrying out procedures, for example, the Pomodoro strategy and giving ambient sound intended to upgrade fixation. By establishing virtual conditions helpful for efficiency, these applications help students in dealing with their time during concentrate on meetings really.

Besides, propensity following applications add to the advancement of predictable and helpful schedules. Stages like Habitica and Streaks permit understudies to set and screen day to day propensities, empowering the development of positive ways of behaving. Whether it's keeping a normal report schedule, remaining hydrated, or taking part in actual activity, these applications give a visual portrayal of progress, cultivating a pride.

The appearance of computerized reasoning has brought shrewd individual partners into the domain of using time productively. Remote helpers like Siri, Google Partner, and Amazon Alexa can be customized to set updates, answer questions, and even perform explicit undertakings. By utilizing voice orders, understudies can proficiently deal with their timetables and access data sans hands, an especially valuable component during feverish periods.

With regards to scholarly exploration and composing, reference the board devices assume a crucial part. Zotero, Mendeley, and EndNote help students in putting together and referring to hotspots for their tasks. These devices smooth out the most common way of gathering, explaining, and referring to references, guaranteeing the scholastic uprightness of their work while saving impressive time in the examination stage.

Language learning applications offer an exceptional road for students hoping to broaden their range of abilities. Stages like Duolingo, Babbel, and Rosetta Stone permit understudies to integrate language learning into their day-to-day schedules. This coordination improves mental capacities as well as gives a useful method for using brief breaks between concentrate on meetings.

Monetary administration applications add to the comprehensive way to deal with students' lives. Stages like Mint, YNAB (You Want a Spending plan), and PocketGuard help understudies in planning, following costs, and defining monetary objectives. This proactive way to deal with monetary administration can lighten pressure and interruptions, permitting understudies to zero in additional eagerly on their scholastic interests.

All in all, the investigation of mechanical devices and applications taking care of students' time usage needs uncovers a rich scene of assets. From planning and errand the board to note-taking, joint effort, and then some, these instruments offer a complex way to deal with upgrading effectiveness and efficiency. It is essential for students to survey their singular inclinations and necessities to choose a customized tool compartment that lines up with their one-of-a-kind scholastic excursion. As innovation keeps on advancing, so too will the amazing chances to refine and enhance time usage procedures, eventually engaging students to explore the intricacies of their scholarly interests no sweat and achievement.

This data could be then utilized in building a customized growth opportunity in future learning exercises utilizing a blend of refined search and customized motors.

Obviously, none of the innovation arrangements is great, however by shutting the criticism circle from a student's exercises back to the arrangement, the nature of answers given to a student will continually get to the next level.

Having that, rather than "sort out yourself" kind of learning, workers could appreciate and encounter really customized learning.

CHAPTER SEVEN

Overcoming Procrastination: Strategies to Stay on Track.

Procrastination is a propensity that plagues many individuals, from understudies to experts. It's the demonstration of deferring or delaying assignments, frequently to the purpose in it causing pressure or damage. While it might appear as though a basic demonstration, there are many justifications for why we delay.

Procrastination is a typical issue that can have serious outcomes, but at the same time a propensity can be survived. By recognizing the motivations behind why we deferral and doing whatever it may take to defeat them, we can work on our efficiency, decrease pressure, and accomplish our objectives.

So, the following time you end up deferring an errand, pause for a minute to consider the reason why you're getting it done and afterward make a move to defeat that deterrent. Keep in mind, it's never beyond any good time to begin!

Here are the reasons people procrastinate

1.Anxiety toward Disappointment: Quite possibly of the most widely recognized reason we delay is dread of disappointment. We might stay away from an undertaking since we're apprehensive we'll do it inadequately or not live up to assumptions.

2.Absence of Inspiration: Some of the time we miss the mark on inspiration to begin an undertaking. We may not see the point or feel overpowered by the size of the assignment.

3.Overpower: When an errand feels too large or complex, deferring beginning it is simple.

4.Hairsplitting: We might maintain that everything should be awesome, which can prompt deferrals as we work to get everything on the money.

5.Absence of Concentration: In the event that we're quickly flustered or experience difficulty concentrating, getting everything rolling on a task can be troublesome.

6.Absence of Lucidity: In the event that we don't have a reasonable comprehension of what we really want to do, we might defer beginning the undertaking until we do.

7.Feeling Worried: While we're feeling anxious or restless, it tends to be difficult to zero in on anything, including the main job.

8.Apathy: At times we delay essentially in light of the fact that we don't want to do the undertaking.

9.Absence of Certainty: In the event that we don't trust in ourselves or our capacities, we might defer beginning an undertaking.

10.Time Usage Issues: Unfortunate using time effectively can prompt postpones in finishing assignments.

At any point do you feel like your review propensities essentially aren't cutting it? Do you consider how you could be performing better in class and on tests? Numerous understudies understand that their secondary school concentrate on propensities isn't extremely compelling in school. This is reasonable, as school is very unique in relation to secondary school. The teachers are less actually involved, classes are greater, tests are worth more, perusing is more serious, and classes are significantly more thorough. That doesn't mean there's anything amiss with you; it simply implies you really want to get familiar with some more powerful review abilities. Luckily, there are numerous dynamic, viable review systems that are demonstrated to be successful in school classes.

This gift offers a few hints on compelling research. Executing these tips into your customary review routine will help you to productively and actually advance course material. Explore different avenues regarding them and discover some that work for you.

Reading is not studying

Just perusing and once again understanding texts or notes isn't effectively captivating in the material. It is essentially re-perusing your notes. Just 'doing' the readings for class isn't contemplating. It is essentially doing the perusing for class. Re-perusing prompts speedy neglecting.

Consider perusing a significant piece of pre-examining, yet learning data requires effectively captivating in the material. Dynamic commitment is the most common way of building significance from text that includes making associations with addresses, framing models, and managing your own learning. Dynamic research doesn't mean featuring or underlining text, re-perusing, or repetition retention. However, these exercises might assist with keeping you participated in the errand, they are not viewed as dynamic concentrating on strategies and are feebly connected with further developed learning.

WHO IS LIKELY TO PROCRASTINATE?

There is no exploration demonstrating that orientation or insight influences one's inclination to linger, however age might have something to do with it. One examination investigation discovers that hesitation tops in the mid-to late twenties, diminishes for the following forty years, and afterward increments again in the sixties. Individuals with sadness, who might have low energy and hold negative considerations about their capacity to finish things, as often as possible dislike dawdling. And afterward there is the fussbudget. Those fussbudgets who set their own guidelines appear to approve of "sloth," however the individuals who have taken on the principles set by others in all actuality do experience difficulty finishing their work. This is on the grounds that they are delicate to the assessments they could get from others — they need to keep away from social dissatisfaction.

STRATEGIES FOR OVERCOMING PROCRASTINATION

Inspect your "shoulds." This applies to "ought's," "musts" and "need to's" also. At the point when we feel committed to another person, we might feel repressed. Change these assertions to "needs," and afterward you take on obligation yourself for doing an errand. As opposed to saying, "I ought to call my child's educator," change it to "I need to call my child's educator."

Take a gander at your reasons judiciously. Truth be told, make up a rundown of the reasons you use which keep you from finishing a task. Then, at that point, inspect each reason and next to it work out a more sensible idea. For instance, "I'm not in that frame of mind" can be reconsidered as "Temperament doesn't take care of business."

Utilize self-inspiring explanations. How we characterize an undertaking can change our inspiration for finishing it. Many individuals rehash expressions to themselves, or even post notes in apparent spots, which prod them on. Evaluate phrases like, "The sooner I'm finished, the sooner I'm free," or "There's never a better time than right now."

Make a plan for the day. Work out a rundown of things you want to do this week (or day, or month) and afterward cross them off, individually, when they are finished. With this rundown, you can see precisely exact thing should be achieved, and you can get a sensation of satisfaction as the rundown gets trimmed down.

Put forth boundaries. On your daily agenda, rank the positions that should be finished arranged by their significance. Beginning with the main, center around just a single occupation at a time.

Separate the assignment into more modest pieces. This is one of the main ways of combatting delaying. Record every one of the means associated with your task and see each step as a sensible work that can completely finish a sensible measure of exertion. Regardless of whether we detest a few obligations, we can deal with them in the event that they last just for a brief time frame.

Check break. We now and then have an unfortunate idea of what amount of time it requires to get done with a responsibility. Instead of overreacting at the prospect that you just have seven days to get that benefit and misfortune articulation together, break the pieces of the assignment down into constant. You might observe that it is just a two-hour work.

Stand firm. Think of yourself an agreement to follow through with a task and sign it. Or on the other hand let a steady companion know that you intend to complete a task by a specific date. Make your task a public undertaking as opposed to remaining quiet about it. Acquiring the help of others and having them consider you responsible aides when you feel obstructed.

Sort out. Ensure you have a perfect workspace and each of your materials before you. Dispense with interruptions like the television booming behind the scenes assuming that you want to think. Caution others that you will be inaccessible (or horrendous) during a specific time.

Deal with your pressure. There are various strategies you can use to manage nervousness: profound breathing, moderate muscle unwinding, perception, actual activity, unwinding tapes, humor and music.

Simply begin. You don't need to hold on until you feel roused to compose that discourse. Simply compose whatever rings a bell, and you can update it later. Indeed, even the longest excursion starts with one little step.

Reward yourself when you achieve a little objective. As opposed to dawdling an entire evening by considering companions, consider a companion just when you have composed a page of the report as an approach to remunerating yourself.

Take a gander at all you have achieved. Instead of rebuffing yourself for not having done what's needed, adopt the more certain strategy of looking at all that you have done. Is the glass half unfilled or half full?

Praise the consummation of your errand. Have a particular prize as a main priority for when your task is done. Go out for supper. Head out to a film. Require an end of the week trip. Host a get-together. The festival ought to be equivalent to your undertaking.

Procrastination is a common challenge faced by many undergraduates, often hindering their academic success and personal growth. Understanding the root causes of procrastination is crucial in developing effective strategies to overcome this habit and maintain a proactive approach to time management. In this discussion, we will delve into the common causes of procrastination among undergraduates and offer practical strategies to help them overcome this challenge.

Practical Strategies to Overcome Procrastination:

Set Realistic Goals:

Establish achievable short-term and long-term goals. Break these goals into smaller tasks, making them more manageable and less overwhelming.

Create a Schedule:

Develop a realistic and structured daily or weekly schedule. Allocate specific time slots for studying, attending classes, and engaging in extracurricular activities.

Prioritize Tasks:

Use techniques such as the Eisenhower Matrix to prioritize tasks based on urgency and importance. Tackle high-priority tasks first and avoid the temptation to procrastinate on essential assignments.

Use Time Management Techniques:

Experiment with time management techniques like the Pomodoro Technique, which involves focused work intervals followed by short breaks. This can enhance productivity and prevent burnout.

Develop a Growth Mindset:

Embrace challenges and view failures as opportunities for growth. Cultivating a growth mindset can reduce the fear of failure, making it easier to tackle tasks without procrastination.

Break Down Tasks:

Divide larger tasks into smaller, more manageable components. Completing these smaller steps provides a sense of accomplishment and progress, reducing the likelihood of procrastination.

Eliminate Distractions:

Identify and minimize potential distractions during study sessions. Turn off notifications, find a quiet study space, and consider using productivity apps that block distracting websites.

Seek Accountability:

Share your goals with friends, family, or classmates who can provide encouragement and accountability. Having a support system can help you stay focused and committed.

Reward Yourself:

Establish a system of rewards for completing tasks. Celebrate achievements, no matter how small, to reinforce positive behavior and motivate continued effort.

Practice Self-Reflection:

Regularly reflect on your progress and identify patterns of procrastination. Understanding the underlying causes can help you develop targeted strategies for improvement.

Conclusion:

Procrastination is a common challenge among undergraduates, but with the right strategies, it can be overcome. By addressing the root causes, setting realistic goals, and implementing effective time management techniques, students can develop a proactive approach to their studies. It's essential to recognize that overcoming procrastination is a gradual process that requires self-awareness, commitment, and continuous effort. Implementing these practical strategies will not only improve academic performance but also foster a proactive and disciplined mindset that can benefit students throughout their academic and professional journeys.

CHAPTER EIGHT

Building Healthy Habits: Integrating Self-Care into Your Routine.

How about we clear up one normal misguided judgment at every turn: Taking care of oneself isn't inseparable from egocentrism or being childish. Taking care of oneself means dealing with yourself so you can be sound, you can be well, you can take care of your business, you can help and really focus on others, and you can do everything you want to and need to achieve in a day.

Taking care of oneself is important for the response to how we can generally well adapt to everyday stressors, it's work pressure. It's the pressure of attempting to stay aware of the speed of day-to-day existence, which innovation has rushed like never before (simply think the number of messages that come flooding into your inbox every day). "Individuals are feeling lonelier and less ready to loosen up and dial back, which causes them to feel more restless and overpowered by even the easiest errands.

What Is Taking care of oneself, and Why Is It Basic for Your Prosperity?

A few associations and scientists adopt a wellbeing focused strategy while characterizing taking care of oneself. The World Wellbeing Association characterizes taking care of oneself as: "the capacity of people, families, and networks to advance wellbeing, forestall infection, keep up with wellbeing, and adapt to sickness and incapacity regardless of the help of a wellbeing worker."

As per this definition, taking care of oneself incorporates everything connected with remaining genuinely solid — including cleanliness, nourishment, and looking for clinical consideration when required. It's all the means an individual can require to oversee stressors in their day-to-day existence and deal with their own wellbeing and prosperity.

What Considers Taking care of oneself, and What Doesn't

It's absolutely impossible to say precisely exact thing considers taking care of oneself since everybody's definition is their own and one of a kind.

The basic decide is that something brings you supported delight over the long haul, Courtney says. What's more, however there are a lot of instances of taking care of oneself that appear to step a scarce difference between a wellbeing improving way of behaving and egocentrism, taking care of oneself doesn't need to be tied in with cushioning your schedule with extravagant encounters or exercises that cost cash (however it unquestionably can).

Consider a manicure or a massage or any other pampering activity. It might seem indulgent, but if the activity helps you de-stress and carve out time for yourself, it counts as self-care, Amsellem says. If weekly manicures or monthly spa days are beyond your means, they will likely add stress to your life in the long run, so there are plenty of other self-care practices you can adopt.

"Self-care does not have to cost anything — it's just doing things you enjoy. And a lot of the things we enjoy or feel fulfilled from cost nothing," Amsellem says. "Stepping outside and taking a deep breath, for example, might be the greatest act of self-care."

Even if you can't spend lots of time and money, Gill Lopez says you can still practice self-care several times a week by turning things you do every day into self-care practices.

Maybe you try being more mindful of your thoughts on your commute, or maybe you find ways to make daily tasks, like showering, more enjoyable. Pick a soap with a scent that you love, and focus on the physical sensations of the shower. Gill Lopez says: What does your shower smell like? What does it sound like? How does the warm water feel on your skin? "For about 10 minutes in the shower, which I have to do anyway, instead of letting my monkey brain run wild, I'm right there," she says.

Daily chores like making your bed in the morning are also examples of self-care — or can be. "This is where that individuality comes into play, because for some people there is no way making a bed feels like self-care — it may just feel like a chore," Amsellem says. But if it helps you claim your day and gives you a sense of accomplishment early on, you'll have that with you even if the rest of the day gets derailed, Amsellem says.

The simple act of making your bed in the morning likely isn't sufficient to account for all your self-care, she says. You may need to routinely devote time and energy to other self-care practices, she adds. "But if there are some days when you feel out of control, on those days, starting the day off doing what you wanted to do for yourself might be one of the biggest forms of self-care you engage in that day."

And sometimes when all of our other self-care plans get thrown out of whack (you worked through your yoga class, your friend canceled your coffee date — we've all been there), it's those small practices of self-care that provide just enough calm to help us get through the day and wake up in a better mood tomorrow.

Instructions to Begin a Taking care of oneself Daily schedule

To get everything rolling with a taking care of oneself everyday practice:

Figure out which exercises give you pleasure, renew your energy, and reestablish your equilibrium.

Begin little by picking one conduct you might want to integrate into your daily practice in the following week.

Develop to rehearsing that conduct consistently for multi week.

Ponder how you feel.

Add more practices when prepared.

Help support through sharing practices from friends and family, a mentor, an authorized proficient (like a specialist or dietitian), or through your medical care plan, local area, or work environment.

Rehearsing taking care of oneself needn't bother with to be a weighty lift right out of the entryway. The following are a couple of thoughts to slide you into your taking care of oneself excursion:

Diary.

Begin every day by focusing on your breath for five minutes and setting expectations for the afternoon.

Have breakfast.

Consider what you're thankful for every evening.

Put your telephone on standalone mode for a half hour before bed every night to set yourself free from the whirlwind of notices.

Call a companion just to make proper acquaintance.

Take up a loosening up side interest.

Pick a sleep time, and stick to it.

Note: In the event that you read this and feel a feeling of crippling or trouble from the difficulties of mounting or laying out a taking care of oneself practice, finding support and support is ideal. There might be hindrances to really focusing on yourself from past injury, emotional well-being issues, or family circumstances that might be making it more testing to get everything rolling. Look for help from confided in guides and conduct wellbeing suppliers (like a specialist), a believed essential consideration specialist, or a dear companion.

The Symbiosis of Healthy Habits and Effective Time Management for Undergraduates.

In the fast-paced world of undergraduate studies, effective time management is often the key to success. As students navigate through lectures, assignments, exams, and perhaps part-time work, the demands on their time can be overwhelming. In this dynamic environment, the incorporation of healthy habits emerges as a critical factor in not only maintaining physical and mental well-being but also optimizing time management. This discussion explores the profound impact of cultivating healthy habits on an undergraduate's ability to manage time efficiently, stay focused, and achieve academic excellence.

Body:

1. Actual Wellbeing and Energy Levels:

Actual wellbeing is the foundation of powerful using time productively. At the point when students focus on their prosperity, they experience expanded energy levels, better fixation, and worked on in general efficiency.

Taking part in customary activity, keeping a fair eating regimen, and guaranteeing satisfactory rest contribute fundamentally to actual wellbeing. Actual work, specifically, has been connected to upgraded mental capability and better mind-set guideline, furnishing understudies with the endurance expected to handle scholastic difficulties.

2. Psychological wellness and Stress The board:

The connection between emotional wellness and using time effectively is perplexing. Persistent pressure and burnout can thwart an understudy's capacity to concentration and take full advantage of their time. Carrying out pressure the executive's strategies, like care contemplation, profound breathing activities, or normal breaks, encourages mental flexibility. At the point when understudies focus on psychological well-being, they establish a climate helpful for successful using time productively and supported scholarly execution.

3. Laying out a Reliable Rest Schedule:

Quality rest is many times underestimated chasing scholastic achievement. Notwithstanding, a very much refreshed mind is more alarm, centered, and equipped for proficient time use. Fostering a reliable rest routine by sticking to standard sleep times and wake-up plans adds to all the more likely using time productively during waking hours. Sufficient rest guarantees that understudies can move toward their examinations with lucidity and life.

4. Sustenance and Mental Capability:

Sustenance assumes an urgent part in mental capability. A very much sustained mind is better prepared to deal with complex undertakings and hold data. By embracing good dieting propensities, for example, consuming a fair eating routine wealthy in supplements, students can improve their mental capacities. This, thus, decidedly influences their capacity to oversee time actually, as they can handle and handle data all the more effectively.

5. Time Usage through Objective Arranged Propensities:

Integrating sound propensities isn't just about physical and mental prosperity; it's likewise about fostering an objective situated outlook. Understudies who develop propensities lined up with their scholar and individual objectives are better prepared to actually deal with their time. For example, saving explicit times for centered concentrate on meetings, coordinating breaks for active work, and laying out a normal that focuses on wellbeing add to a proactive way to deal with using time productively.

6. The Job of Sound Breaks:

As opposed to the conviction that consistent work prompts ideal efficiency, integrating solid breaks is critical for supported focus. Brief breaks during concentrate on meetings, including exercises like extending, strolling, or profound breathing, can revive the brain. These breaks forestall burnout, upgrade center, and add to compelling time portion by keeping a harmony among work and unwinding.

7. Using Innovation Carefully:

In the computerized age, innovation is necessary to understudy life. In any case, careful utilization of innovation is fundamental for keeping up with sound propensities and proficient using time effectively. Defining limits on screen time, utilizing efficiency applications to sort out errands, and integrating innovation free periods for rest and unwinding add to a decent and successful way to deal with using time productively.

8. Social Associations and Using time effectively:

Sound propensities reach out past individual prosperity to social associations. Keeping an encouraging group of people of companions and participating in friendly exercises is essential for psychological well-being. By encouraging positive connections, understudies establish a social climate that helps pressure decrease. This, thusly, takes into consideration better using time effectively as understudies can move toward their scholastic obligations with an unmistakable and centered outlook.

9. Building Versatility and Flexibility:

Sound propensities add to the advancement of flexibility and versatility, essential ascribes for exploring the difficulties of undergrad life. Tough people can quickly return from difficulties, staying away from delayed times of hesitation or demotivation. The capacity to adjust to changing conditions empowers understudies to change their time usage methodologies progressively, guaranteeing proceeded with outcome in their scholarly interests.

10. All encompassing Way to deal with Self-awareness:

The fuse of sound propensities is innately connected to an all-encompassing way to deal with self-improvement. Students who focus on their prosperity perceive the interconnectedness of physical, mental, and close to home wellbeing. This all-encompassing viewpoint develops a proactive and deliberate way to deal with using time productively, where every part of their prosperity adds to the general streamlining of their scholarly excursion.

Conclusion:

All in all, the cooperative connection between sound propensities and compelling using time productively is a major part of undergrad achievement. By focusing on physical and mental prosperity, laying out predictable schedules, and encouraging an objective situated attitude, understudies can establish a climate helpful for proficient time usage. The advantages stretch out past scholarly execution to envelop by and large self-awareness, flexibility, and versatility.

As students explore the intricacies of their scholastic process, perceiving the basic job of solid propensities in using time productively turns into a foundation of practical achievement. By embracing a comprehensive way to deal with prosperity, understudies improve their scholarly exhibition as well as establish the groundwork for a reasonable and satisfying life past the homeroom. As the expression goes, a solid brain in a sound body, when applied to the setting of undergrad life, turns into the impetus for powerful using time productively and a prospering scholastic encounter.

CHAPTER NINE.

Reflecting and Adapting: Continuous Improvement in Time Management.

Dominating Using time effectively: A Diagram for Ceaseless Improvement in Undergraduate Life.

Time is a valuable asset, particularly for students who shuffle scholastic obligations, extracurricular exercises, and social commitment. The capacity to oversee time really is an expertise that improves scholarly execution as well as sets the establishment for a fruitful and healthy lifestyle. In this article, we will investigate the idea of ceaseless improvement in using time productively for students, giving significant methodologies to assist understudies with advancing their timetables and take full advantage of their school insight.

Grasping the Significance of Using time effectively:

Using time effectively is something beyond a trendy expression; a basic expertise can fundamentally influence scholastic achievement and individual prosperity. Students frequently face a huge number of requests, from going to addresses and finishing tasks to partaking in clubs and keeping a public activity. Viable using time effectively permits understudies to explore these requests with proficiency and decrease pressure.

The Constant Improvement Mentality:

Constant improvement is a mentality that includes making little, gradual changes over the long run to upgrade execution and accomplish long haul objectives. Applying this outlook to using time effectively recognizes that there is generally opportunity to get better and that the excursion towards ideal time use is continuous. This is the way students can take on and embrace the consistent improvement mentality:

Self-Reflection:

Start by pondering your ongoing time usage rehearses. Recognize regions where you succeed and perspectives that need improvement. Is it true or not that you are investing an excess of energy in unnecessary exercises? Do you battle with dawdling? Genuine self-appraisal is the most vital move towards significant change.

Put forth Reasonable Objectives:

Lay out both present moment and long-haul objectives connected with using time productively. These objectives ought to be explicit, quantifiable, feasible, pertinent, and time-bound (Savvy). For instance, a momentary objective could be to finished all tasks a day on time for the following month, while a drawn-out objective could include keeping a reliable report plan all through the semester.

Focus on Errands:

Not all errands are made equivalent. Figure out how to separate among dire and significant assignments. Use instruments like the Eisenhower Grid to classify assignments into four quadrants: pressing and significant, significant however not earnest, critical yet not significant, and neither dire nor significant. Center around errands in the initial two quadrants to amplify efficiency.

Time Obstructing:

Carry out the procedure of time obstructing to designate explicit blocks of time to various exercises. This makes an organized daily practice and forestalls performing multiple tasks, which can be counterproductive. Devote blocks of time to addresses, examining, mingling, and taking care of oneself, guaranteeing a reasonable way to deal with your day.

Reasonable Techniques for Consistent Improvement:

Now that we comprehend the mentality behind consistent improvement, we should dig into commonsense systems that students can embrace to upgrade their time usage abilities:

Use an Organizer or Schedule:

Put resources into an actual organizer or utilize computerized devices like Google Schedule to monitor tasks, cutoff times, and responsibilities. Consistently update and survey your organizer to remain coordinated and stay away from last-minute packing.

Separate Assignments:

Huge undertakings can be overpowering, prompting delaying. Separate tasks into more modest, more sensible assignments. For example, rather than expecting to finish a whole exploration paper at a time, put forth objectives to investigate sources, frame the paper, and compose explicit segments on various days.

Wipe out Time Killers:

Recognize and take out exercises that consume time without contributing altogether to your objectives. This could incorporate unreasonable virtual entertainment use, staring at the Network programs, or participating in ineffective discussions. Consider utilizing applications or site blockers to restrict interruptions during concentrate on meetings.

Figure out how to Say No:

While extracurricular exercises are important, overcommitting can prompt burnout and compromise scholarly execution. Figure out how to express no to extra obligations when your timetable is full. Focus on better standards without compromise in your responsibilities.

Consistently Evaluate and Change:

Constant improvement includes consistently surveying your time usage systems and making changes depending on the situation. Assess what's functioning admirably and what needs refinement. Be adaptable and open to attempting new ways to deal with find what suits your singular inclinations and necessities.

Consolidate Breaks:

Perceive the significance of breaks in keeping up with efficiency and concentration. Use procedures like the Pomodoro Method, which includes 25 minutes of centered work followed by a 5-minute break. This can forestall burnout and keep a manageable degree of energy over the course of the day.

Look for Criticism:

Make it a point to input from companions, tutors, or teachers with respect to your time usage abilities. They might give significant bits of knowledge and thoughts in view of their encounters. Productive criticism can be an impetus for positive change.

The Advantages of Persistent Improvement in Using time productively:

Embracing persistent improvement in using time effectively can yield various advantages for college understudies:

Improved Scholastic Execution:

Successful using time productively permits understudies to commit engaged and quality chance to their examinations. This, thusly, can prompt superior comprehension obviously materials, better maintenance of data, and higher scholarly execution.

Decreased Pressure and Nervousness:

Complying with time constraints, remaining coordinated, and having an unmistakable arrangement can essentially lessen pressure and uneasiness levels. The feeling of control that accompanies successful using time productively adds to by and large prosperity.

Adjusted Way of life:

Constant improvement in using time effectively empowers understudies to work out some kind of harmony between scholarly obligations and individual life. This equilibrium is urgent for keeping up with psychological well-being, encouraging connections, and participating in exercises past the scholastic domain.

Groundwork for Future Difficulties:

The abilities created through nonstop improvement in using time productively are adaptable to different parts of life and future vocation tries. Businesses esteem people who can effectively deal with their time, fulfill time constraints, and stay versatile in powerful conditions.

Taking steps to improve your time management skills has numerous advantages. More than being efficient at work, effective time management can help you significantly reduce stress and improve your work-life balance.

In succinct;

Dominating using time productively is a continuous cycle that requires devotion, self-reflection, and a promise to nonstop improvement. By embracing a proactive mentality, laying out sensible objectives, and carrying out useful procedures, students can improve their timetables, upgrade scholarly execution, and develop a reasonable and satisfying school insight. The excursion towards successful using time productively is definitely not a one-size-fits-all undertaking, so understudies ought to investigate various ways to deal with find what turns out best for them. Keep in mind, the way to progress lies in overseeing time as well as in consistently further developing the manner time is made due.

www.ingramcontent.com/pod-product-compliance
Lightning Source LLC
Chambersburg PA
CBHW050307230526
45471CB00005B/2063